MW00509440

The Perfect Keto Diet

Healthy Recipes for a Daily Meal Plan!

New LifeStyle

Table of Contents

INTRODUCTION

You have probably been told that your body is designed to work mainly on carbs. Carbs provide energy to our bodies for daily work, exercise, walking, or doing routine housework all the time. We consume carbs for energy, but most of us do not realize that carbs are not the only source of generating energy in a body. Other substances, like fats, are also effective fuel.

The keto diet emphasizes cutting carbs from your diet and includes a sufficient amount of fats. It is not a fad diet like many others. It has been around since 1920 and has many success stories of improved healthy lifestyle and weight loss. The keto diet is all about proper management of body fuel. Most people's main question is how to manage a proper keto diet and how their body will work during the diet.

First of all, you have to understand keto.

The keto diet is high in fat and lower in carbs. The human body uses carbohydrates as the primary source of fuel. When fats replace the carbs, the body enters a specific metabolic state known as "ketosis."During ketosis, the body uses stored fat as fuel, which aids in weight loss. The keto diet also has many health benefits like management of diabetes, lowering cholesterol, improving mental clarity, reducing PCOS, and lowering the risk of cancer, as well as improving heart health.

What is the Keto Diet?

The keto diet is a high-fat, proportionate-protein, and low-carbohydrate diet. The diet forces the body to burn bad fats in the place of carbohydrates. Generally, the carbs contained in food are changed into glucose, which are used for fueling brain function. When there are limited carbohydrates in the diet, the liver converts fats into ketones and fatty acids, which travel to the brain and replace glucose as useable energy.

Nowadays, there are many weight-loss diets. Low-carb, high-protein plans such as the paleo, South Beach, and Atkins diets are often confused with the keto diet, but they are actually quite different. The actual keto diet is the healthiest and most effective option.

How Does the Keto Diet Work?

The keto diet's primarily purpose is to strengthen your body using a different type of energy. As a replacement for the sugars in carbs, the keto diet relies on ketone bodies. Ketone bodies are energy forms that the human liver produces from fats.

Burning fat seems like a perfect way to lose weight, but forcing the liver to make ketone bodies is complex. It requires consuming less than 20 to 50 grams of carbohydrates per day, and it usually takes a few days to reach a state of ketosis. On the other hand, you should avoid over-eating because too much protein can delay the ketosis process.

Benefits of the Keto Diet

The keto diet has numerous benefits, some of which are listed below:

- **Weight loss**

The keto diet helps to support weight loss in many ways. It boosts metabolism and reduces hunger. Keto diets contain foods that satisfy cravings and reduce hunger-stimulating hormones. For these reasons, the keto diet helps to reduce hunger and aids in weight loss.

- **Improves skin**

There are many causes of acne. Some are directly linked to diet and blood sugar. The keto diet helps to decrease insulin levels, which is the main cause of skin cell growth, sebum, and androgens, for acne eruptions. The keto diet helps to improve blood circulation in the body, enhancing skin health and reducing acne.

- **Reduces the risk of certain cancers**

Many researchers have endorsed the keto diet for the prevention of certain types of cancers or even to treat certain diseases. The keto diet is a safe and suitable hormone treatment instead of chemotherapy and radiation therapy for certain cancers. It grounds more oxidative pressure in cancer cells than in healthy cells, causing them to die.

- **Improves heart health**

Following the ketogenic diet encourages healthy food choices. Eating healthy fats like avocados instead of beef can help lower cholesterol levels. Many people experience a major drop in levels of total cholesterol, LDL, and triglycerides, and an increase in HDL or "good" cholesterol. Lowering cholesterol levels reduces the risk of heart complications.

- **Stimulates brain function**

The ketones generated during the keto diet provide neuro-protective aid, by which they can strengthen and protect the brain and nerve cells. For this reason, a keto diet helps prevent and manage conditions like Alzheimer's disease and improves brain function.

- **Diminishes seizures**

The ketosis produced from the keto diet can help to diminish seizures in people with epilepsy, mainly those peoples who have not responded to other treatments. The keto diet has the most positive effect on children with seizures. The ketogenic diet reduces epilepsy symptoms by several different mechanisms.

- **Improves PCOS/PCOD symptoms in women**

Polycystic ovary syndrome (PCOS) or polycystic ovary disorder (PCOD) is a hormonal condition that leads to polycystic ovaries, ovulatory dysfunction, and the release of male hormones. A high-carb diet can cause opposing effects in people with PCOS, such as skin problems and weight gain. A keto diet is a well-managed and proper portion diet, which helps to manageseveral signs of PCOS/PCOD, including hormone imbalance, weight loss, levels of fasting insulin, and ratios of luteinizing hormone (LH) and follicle-stimulating hormone (FSH).

Types of Keto Diets:

It may blow your mind to know that there isn't just one type of keto diet. There are actually four conventional methods to the keto diet, which are:

- Standard keto diet
- Targeted keto diet
- Cyclical keto diet
- High-proteinketo diet

Each type of diet can help you burn fat, lose weight, and balance blood sugar levels, but they are all are different in their detailed objectives and benefits.

- **The Standard Ketogenic Diet**

The standard ketogenic diet (SKD) is one of the most common types of the ketogenic diet. It is best for beginners who want to lose body fat or for those with insulin resistance. Following is the protocol for SKD.

- High fat intake, roughly 70 to 75% of total calories
- Proper protein intake is 0.8 grams of protein per pound.
- Consumption of 20 to 50 grams of total carbs per day, or less than 5% of total calories.

- **The High-Protein Ketogenic Diet**

The high-protein ketogenic diet is similar to SKD but with extra protein. The main principle is to consume extra protein to build muscle. On the high-protein keto diet, you will follow these rules:

- 35% of calories from protein
- 60% of the calories from fat
- 5% of calories from carbohydrates

This technique is popular with weightlifters, bodybuilders, or those who need more protein in their diet.

- **The Cyclical Keto Diet**

The cyclical keto diet (CKD) involves eating a low-carb diet some days, followed by a high-carb diet for a day or two.

On the CKD, a person will alternate between two stages. The first is a standard ketogenic diet phase with a carb-loading period. The high-carb period can last from 24 to 48 hours. During the carb-loading period, approximately 70%

of calories will come from carbs. For the next week, the diet will look like this:

1. Standard ketogenic diet phase (five days):
- 70 to 75% of calories from fat
- 20 to 25% of calories from protein
- 5% of calories from carbs
2. Carb-loading period (two days):
- 70% of calories from carbs
- 20 to 25% of calories from protein
- 5 to 10% of calories from fat

The CKD is best for athletes and bodybuilders to maximize fat loss while building lean muscles.

- **The Targeted Ketogenic Diet (TKD)**

The targeted ketogenic diet (TKD) focuses on carbs being ingested around your workouts. This is ideal for supporting exercise performance by fueling muscles with glycogen during the workout.

TKD aims to consume 25 to 50 grams of carbs 30 minutes to an hour before a workout. The TKD is a mixture of the SKD and the CKD. It allows you to train at high strength at the gym but doesn't force you out of ketosis for an extended time.

In the TKD diet, the following rules should be considered:

- **Fructose and galactose should be avoided** because they go directly to your liver and are converted into glucose, lactate, glycogen, and lipids.

- **Dextrose and glucose are the best types to eat** because they go to your muscles to restock glycogen stores.

What You Can and Can't Eat in the Keto Diet

The keto diet is well-portioned and complete, but you need to know what to eat and what not to eat. Sotake a few minutes to learn what the best choices for your health are.

- **Carbs (5 to 10% daily caloric intake):**

The approximate grams of carbs per day, based on a 2,000-calorie diet, are 40. You should target high-fiber, water-rich fruits and vegetables to naturally enhance hydration and keep your digestive system healthy.

Some good examples of carb food choices are:

- Tomatoes
- Eggplant
- Asparagus
- Broccoli
- Cauliflower
- Spinach
- Green Beans
- Cucumber
- Bell peppers
- Kale
- Zucchini

- Celery
- Brussels sprouts

- **Protein (10 to 20% of daily caloric intake):**

The approximate grams of carbs per day based on a 2,000-calorie diet are 70. If you eat extra fat and less protein than suggested, your body will turn to muscle tissue as fuel. This will lower your total muscle mass and the number of calories you burn at rest. The proper proportion of protein is necessary for the maintenance of your weight and health.

Some good examples of protein food choices are:

- Chicken
- Turkey
- Venison
- Beef
- Salmon
- Sardines
- Tuna
- Shrimp
- Lamb
- Eggs
- Natural cheeses
- Whole milk plain Greek yogurt
- Whole milk ricotta cheese
- Whole milk cottage cheese
- Parmesan cheese

- **Fat (70 to 80% of daily caloric intake):**

The approximate grams of carbs per day based on a 2,000-calorie diet are 165. A higher-fat diet can lessen cravings and levels of appetite-stimulating hormones, insulin, and ghrelin. In the keto diet, always go for full-fat without worrying about dietary cholesterol. When consuming a large amount of calories from fat, it's critical to make choices that are less likely to block your arteries.

Some good examples of fat food choices are as follows:

- Olive oil
- Avocado oil
- Olives
- Avocados
- Flaxseeds
- Chia seeds
- Pumpkin seeds
- Sesame seeds
- Hemp hearts
- Coconuts
- Nuts
- Natural nut butter
- Olive oil

What Food to Avoid on a Keto Diet:

It is easier to stay within the macro-nutrient structure by staying clear of these foods:

- Lentils, beans, peas
- Peanuts
- Rice
- Pasta
- Oatmeal
- Artificial sweeteners and sugars
- Sugary beverages, like soda and juices
- Traditional snack foods, like potato chips and crackers
- Some fruits, except for lemons, tomatoes, and berries
- Starchy vegetables like corn and potatoes
- Trans fats, like margarine or other hydrogenated fats
- Alcohols, like wine, beer, and sweetened cocktails
- Beverage cans

How to Eat Keto Food When Dining Out

If you are planning to go out for dinner or a party andwant to maintain a low-carb lifestyle, don't worry. The low-carb keto diet works anywhere. Here are some excellent tips:

- **Plan ahead**

Most restaurants have their menu available online. If you are new to keto and anxious about your food choices, why not plan it in advance? Scan the menu for keto-friendly options that are sugar-free and delightful. You can request starches to be left off the dish, so it is perfect for your keto or low-carb routine.

- **Exclude the starch from the food**

Skip the bread. Pass on the pasta. Eliminate the potatoes. Refuse the rice. Keep temptation off your plate without the starchy dishes. Most restaurants will substitute a salad or veggies for the starch. Go for them. Use lettuce wraps instead of buns or bread on your sandwiches.

- **Add healthy fat to your food**

Restaurant meals are often low in fat, making it hard to feel satisfied without eating carbs, but this problem can be resolved by adding extra fat to a standard offering:

- Go for extra butter and melt it on meat and veggies.
- Request olive oil and vinegar and drizzle the oil generously on salads and your meal.
- Choose heavy cream for your tea or coffee.

- **Choose drinks wisely**

The best beverages are water, tea, coffee, or sparkling water. Avoid alcoholic beverages. If you are tempted by an alcoholic drink, go for champagne, dry wine, or light beer with club soda.

- **Dessert**

If you are hungry or tempted to get a sweet or dessert, go for a cheese plate, berries with heavy cream, or some coffee. Sometimes cream in your coffee is enough to satisfy.

- **Eating at buffet restaurants**

The loveliness of buffets is that there are plenty of choices, including keto and low-carb dishes.

- **Set rules for eating before leaving the table**

Before walking through many attractive offerings take a moment and re-commit to resisting the biggest offenders. Be thoughtful. Be deliberate. And don't forget the primary rule: If you cheat on your diet, you are only hurting yourself. You'll feel so much better afterwards if you stay true to your commitment.

- **Focus on vegetables, protein, and fats**

Focus on all the healthy food you can enjoy: salad, seafood, and vegetable platters can be very satisfying, and you can generally find some healthy fats to add like olive oil, butter, and cheese. If you don't see them, ask the waiter to bring some for you.

- **Don't overfill your plate**

Plan to leave free space or "breathing room" on your plate and don'tcrowd it with food. If you're going to try many things, start with tiny servings of each dish. You can go back for more food if you are still feeling hungry.

- **Take your time and enjoy your companions**

Focus on enjoying the company and the conversation. Have your water or sip your coffee and enjoy chatting. Sometimes there is a pause before you feel satisfied, so don't rush back for seconds if you're trying to lose weight.

Limitations of the Keto Diet

The ketogenic diet may have a variety of health benefits. However, staying on the ketogenic diet for long periods can be bad for you, including an increased risk of the following health problems:

- Kidney stones
- Excess protein in the blood
- Mineral and vitamin deficiencies
- Fat build-up in the liver

The keto diet can also cause a side effect known as the "keto flu." These adverse effects include:

- Constipation
- Low blood sugar
- Nausea
- Fatigue
- Vomiting
- Headaches

These symptoms are particularly prevalent at the beginning as the body adjusts troits new energy source.

Some people should avoid the keto diet, including:

- People with diabetes who are insulin-dependent
- People who have eating disorders
- People who have kidney disease or pancreatitis
- Pregnant women
- Breastfeeding mothers

It is essential to discuss any proposed diet plan with your doctor and dietitian, especially for people who are managing a health problem or disease.

Let's start with the recipes, folks!

Breakfast Keto Recipes

Eggs and Bacon in Avocado Boats

6 servings

Preparation time: 25 minutes

Ingredients

- 6 large Eggs
- 4 Bacon slices
- 3 avocados
- 2 ½ tbsp chopped chives
- 1 tsp smoked paprika powder
- Pepper to taste
- Salt to taste

Directions

- Preheat the oven at 360°F.
- Cut avocadoes in halves and pitted. Scoop out some flesh in a bowl.
- Place the halved avocados in the greased baking tray.
- Crack an egg in each half avocado center.
- Sprinkle the salt, pepper, and smoked paprika powder as per your taste. You can adjust spices as per your taste.
- Diced the bacon slices and sprinkle them on the top of the avocado filling.

- Bake the avocado boats for 14-16 minutes or until set.
- Garnish with freshly chopped chives and enjoy yummy avocado boats with family and friends.

Smoked Salmon with scrambled eggs

6 servings

Preparation time: 30 minutes

Ingredients

- 6 oz smoked salmon, diced
- 1 cup Sour Cream
- 12 large eggs
- 3 tbsp butter
- 3tbsp freshly chopped dill
- Pepper to taste
- Salt to taste

Directions

- Crack the eggs in the bowl and whisk them well.
- Add sour cream, salt pepper in the bowl and mix well with eggs.
- Melt the butter in a pan over medium heat and add eggs. Stir the eggs quickly which form a scramble.
- Cook eggs barely for 2-3 minutes until barely set.
- Remove the pan from heat and stir in the salmon.
- Garnish with freshly chopped dill and serve.

Tofu Scramble with Mushroom and Kale

6 servings

Preparation time: 30 minutes

Ingredients

- 1 ½ cup white mushrooms
- 3 tbsp Ghee
- 4 cloves of Garlic
- 24 oz firm tofu
- 9 eggs
- ¾ cup Kale
- Salt to taste
- Pepper to taste

Directions

- Cut white mushroom and Kale into thin slices and crumbled the tofu. Set the ingredient aside.
- Over medium heat, melt the ghee.
- Sauté the mushrooms for 5 minutes until they are tender.
- Add the garlic and cook for a minute.
- Stir in the tofu and cook for 6 minutes.
- Add seasoning to the mushrooms and tofu to taste.
- Add kale to the pan and mix well, cook the kale for 5 minutes until softened.
- In a bowl crack the eggs.

- Pour the whisked eggs over the kale and stir well with a spatula until scrambled.
- Remove the pan until eggs are fully scrambled and no runnier after minutes and serve hot.

Egg and Bacon Quesadillas

6 servings

Preparation time: 30 minutes

Ingredients

- 12 low carb tortilla shells
- 8 eggs
- 1 cup water
- 5 tbsp butter
- 2 cups grated Swiss cheese
- 2 cup grated cheddar cheese
- 10 bacon slices
- 2 small onions
- 2 tbsp parsley

Directions

- Boil the eggs over medium heat for 10 minutes.
- Transfer the eggs into iced cold water for easy shell peeling. Chop the boiled eggs finely.
- Fry the bacon on medium heat in the pan for few minutes until crispy and golden.
- Chop the crispy bacon. Sauté the chopped onions in the remaining grease of bacon for 2 minutes and set aside.
- Melt 1 tbsp butter over medium heat in the pan. Place the tortilla shell on the butter for crispiness.

- Sprinkle some Swiss cheese over the tortilla.
- Add chopped boil eggs, bacon, and onions over the cheese and topped with the cheddar cheese.
- Cover the stuffing with another tortilla shell.
- Cook for few seconds and flip the quesadilla carefully in the pan.
- Remove the crispy and yummy quesadilla to the plate and garnish with parsley. Repeat the cooking for other tortillas and serve warm.

Cinnamon cream with Almond waffles

4 servings

Preparation time: 25 minutes approximately

Ingredients

For Waffles:

- 3 tbsp melted butter
- 1 cup unsweetened Almond milk
- 5 large eggs
- ¼ tsp liquid stevia
- ½ tsp baking powder
- 1 cup almond flour

For Cinnamon cream:

- 6 oz softened cream cheese
- 1tsp cinnamon powder
- 3 tbsp brown sugar
- 1 ½ tbsp cinnamon

Directions

- Combine cream cheese with swerving brown sugar, cinnamon powder and mix well until smooth.
- Cover the cream and place it in the refrigerator and chill.

- For waffles, whisk eggs, with butter and almond milk.
- Add Stevie and baking powder to the egg mixture.
- Stir in the almond flour and mix well until no lumps.
- Rest the batter for 5 minutes to thicken.
- Spray the waffle iron with cooking spray. Add a ladle or ¼ cup of waffle batter and cook according to instruction as per waffle iron manufacturer until golden.
- Make waffles from all the batter.
- Slice the waffles into the quarter and apply chilled cinnamon cheese cream spread between two waffles and serve.

Pesto Mug cakes with bacon and cheese

4 servings

Preparation time: 8 minutes

Ingredients

For Muffins

- ½ cup Flax meal
- 2 eggs
- 4 tbsp pesto
- 4tbsp heavy cream
- ½ cup Almond flour
- Salt to taste
- Pepper to taste

For filling

- 4tbsp cream cheese
- 1 large sliced avocado
- 4 Bacon slices

Directions

- In a bowl mix the dry ingredients for muffins.
- Add heavy cream and pesto and whisk well with a fork.
- Add salt and pepper to taste.
- Divide the muffin mix into four ramekins.

- Place the ramekins in the microwave for 60-90 seconds.
- Cool the muffins slightly before filling.
- Cook bacon over medium heat until crispy. Soak all excess fat in the paper towel and set bacon aside.
- Invert the muffins onto the plate and crosswise cut in half.
- Spread the cream cheese topped with bacon and avocado slices and assemble in form of sandwiches. Serve warm.

Ricotta Pancakes with cream

6 servings

Preparation time: 20 minutes approximately

Ingredients

- 1 ½ cup Almond flour
- 1 tsp baking powder
- 3 tbsp erythritol
- 1 tsp salt
- 1 cup coconut milk
- 3 large eggs
- 1 ½ cup heavy whipping cream

Directions

- In a bowl add almond flour, baking powder, erythritol, and salt and whisk well.
- Blend the eggs in a processor for 30 minutes.
- Add ricotta cheese and process the blender again.
- Process the mixture until smooth and creamy.
- Pour the creamy egg mixture into the dry mix and combine well.
- Heat the pan over medium heat and pour the spoon full of mixture into the hot pan and cook for 1 minute.
- Flip the pancake and cook for 1 minute.

- Remove the pancake to the plate and repeat the process for other pancakes.
- Serve the pancakes topped with whipping cream. Yummy.

Crispy Pancetta salad with Kale Frittata

6 servings

Preparation time: 25 minutes

Ingredients

- 9 Pancetta slices
- 6 tomatoes
- 1 large cucumber
- 1 medium red onion
- ¼ cup Balsamic vinegar
- 10 eggs
- 1 ¼ bunch of Kale
- Salt to taste
- Pepper to taste
- 6 tbsp olive oil
- 1 large white onion
- 2 clove garlic.

Directions

- Cook pancetta in a pan over medium heat until crispy for about 4 minutes.
- Chopped cook pancetta finely.
- Diced the tomatoes, dressed and sliced the cucumber, slice the onions, minced the garlic, and chop the kale finely, and set aside.

- In a bowl whisk vinegar, salt, Olive oil, and pepper for dressing the salad.
- Combine the salad veggies in a salad bowl and drizzled them with the dressing.
- Toss the salad well to coal dressing evenly.
- Top the salad with pancetta.
- Preheat oven over 360°F.
- Crack eggs in a bowl and whisk well with parmesan cheese, salt, and pepper.
- Heat the olive oil in a pan and sauté onion garlic. Add kale and season with salt and pepper to taste.
- Cook for about 2 minutes until kale softens.
- Pour the egg mixture all over and cook for 4 minutes. Sprinkle the cheese on the top and transfer it to the oven.
- Bake the eggs for 5 minutes until brown on top
- Remove the frittata and slide it onto a warm platter. Cut frittata into slices and serve with pancetta salad.

Zucchini carrot bread

6 servings

Preparation time: 70 minutes

Ingredients

- 1 ½ cup shredded zucchini
- 1 ½ cup shredded carrots
- ½ cup coconut flour
- 1 tsp vanilla extract
- 8 eggs
- 1 tsp baking soda
- 1 ½ tbsp coconut oil
- 1 tbsp cinnamon powder
- ½ tsp salt
- ½ cup Greek yogurt
- 1 tsp apple cider vinegar
- ½ tsp nutmeg powder

Directions

- Preheat the oven to 350°F.
- Mix the coconut flour, vanilla extract, eggs, coconut oil, baking soda, cinnamon, salt vinegar, nutmeg, Greek yogurt, mix them well.
- Squeeze off the zucchini water and add in the bread mix.
- Add shredded carrots and mix.

- Grease the bread loaf pan and pour the batter into it.
- Bake the bread for 55 minutes.
- Remove the bread and cool for 5 minutes.
- You can have the yummy bread as sandwich, toast or serve with salads and soups.

Lunch Keto Recipes

Roasted Capers Chicken Breasts

4 servings

Preparation time: 65 minutes approximately

Ingredients

- 1 cups chicken broth
- 1 tbsp fresh parsley, chopped
- 1 tbsp butter
- 1 medium lemon, sliced
- 2 chicken breasts, halved
- Salt and black pepper to taste
- ¼ cup almond flour
- 2 tbsp olive oil
- 1 tbsp capers, rinsed

Directions

- Preheat oven to 350ºF.

- Roast lemon for 25 minutes on the parchment paper-lined baking tray until the rind gets brown.

- Pound the chicken with a rolling pin to flatten about ½-inch thickness.

- Seasoned the chicken with spices and dredge the chicken in the almond flour on each side.

- Lightly tap to shake off any excess flour. Set aside.

- Heat the olive oil in a pan over medium heat. Fry the chicken on both sides until golden brown, for about 8 minutes.

- Pour the broth into the pan and boil until it becomes thick in consistency around 12 minutes.

- Stir in the capers, butter, and roasted lemons and simmer on low heat for 10 minutes.

- Pour the sauce over the chicken and garnish it with parsley to serve.

Turkey Pie with Rosemary

6 servings

Preparation time: 40 minutes +chilling time

Ingredients

- 2 ½ cups chicken stock
- ½ cup kale, chopped
- ½ cup butternut squash, chopped
- ½ cup cheese, grated
- 1 ½ cup turkey meat, cooked, chopped
- Salt and black pepper to taste
- 1 tbsp fresh rosemary, chopped
- ¼ tsp smoked paprika
- ¼ tsp xanthan gum

For the crust
- 2 cups almond flour
- A pinch of salt
- 1 egg
- ¼ cup butter
- ¼ tsp xanthan gum
- ¼ cup cheddar cheese

Directions

- Set a greased pot over medium heat.

- Cook turkey and squash and for 10 minutes.

- Add stock to the pot cheese, rosemary, black pepper, smoked paprika, kale, and salt.

- In a bowl, mix ½ cup stock from the pot with ¼ teaspoon xanthan gum, and transfer to the pot; set aside.

- In another bowl, stir flour, ¼ teaspoon xanthan gum, and salt.

- Add the butter, cheddar cheese, and egg and knead to form a pie crust.

- Shape the dough into a ball, wrap it in plastic foil, and refrigerate for 30 minutes.

- Spray a baking dish with cooking spray. Sprinkle pie filling on the bottom. Set the dough and roll it into a circle.

- Top the filling with the circle. Make sure that dough is well pressed and seal edges.

- Set in an oven at 350ºF, and bake for 35 minutes. Allow the pie to cool, and enjoy.

Baked Pork Sausage

6 servings

Preparation time: 50 minutes

Ingredients

- 2 lb pork sausages
- 3 large tomatoes, cut in rings
- 3 cloves garlic, minced
- 2 bay leaves
- 3 tbsp olive oil
- 3 tbsp balsamic vinegar
- 1 red bell pepper, sliced
- 1 yellow bell pepper, sliced
- 1 green bell pepper, sliced
- 1 sprig thyme, chopped
- 1 sprig rosemary, chopped

Directions

- Preheat oven to 350ºF.
- Grease the baking pan.
- In a pan, arrange the tomatoes and bell peppers. Sprinkle with thyme, rosemary, garlic, olive oil, and balsamic vinegar.
- Top the sausages over veggies.
- Bake the sausages for 20 minutes.

- Remove the pan, shake it a bit, and turn the sausages over with a spoon.

- Cooked again for 25 minutes or until the sausages have browned to the desired color.

- Serve with the veggie and cooking sauce.

Pork with bacon Wrappings

4 servings

Preparation time: 40 minutes

Ingredients

- 4 bacon slices
- 1 tbsp fresh parsley, chopped
- ¼ cup onions, chopped
- 2 garlic cloves, minced
- 1 lb pork tenderloin, sliced
- 10 oz canned diced tomatoes
- ½ cup vegetable stock
- Salt and black pepper to taste
- ½ tsp Italian seasoning
- ½ cup ricotta cheese
- 2tbsp coconut oil
- 2 tbsp Parmesan cheese, grated

Directions

- Pound the meat until flatten.

- Place the bacon slices on top of each piece and spread the parsley, ricotta cheese, and Parmesan cheese between them.

- Roll each flattened pork piece and secure it with a toothpick.

- Set a pan over medium heat and warm oil. Cook the pork rolls until browned.

- Add garlic and onions to the pan and cook for 5 minutes.

- Place in the stock and cook for 3 minutes. Remove toothpicks from the rolls and return to the pan.

- Stir well in pepper, salt, tomatoes, and Italian seasoning.

- Bring to a boil, reduce the heat, and cook for 20 minutes covered.

- Plate the wraps to serve.

Red Cabbage Salad with Stuffed Pork

6 Servings

Preparation Time: 40 minutes + marinating time

Ingredients

- 2 tbsp mustard
- 1 head red cabbage, shredded
- ¾ cup + 4 tbsp olive oil
- 1 cup fresh cilantro, chopped
- 2 tsp dried oregano
- Salt and black pepper to taste
- 2 tsp cumin
- 6 pork loin steaks
- 3 pickles, chopped
- 6 ham slices
- 8 Swiss cheese slices
- Zest and juice from 3 limes
- 3 garlic cloves, minced
- 2 tbsp vinegar
- Salt to taste

Directions

- In a food processor, add lime zest, ¾ cup oil, oregano, cumin, cilantro, lime juice, garlic, salt, and pepper, and smooth foam paste.
- Rub the steaks with the mixture.

- Place in the fridge for 2 hours to marinate.

- Split the pickles, mustard, cheese, and ham on them, roll, and secure with toothpicks.

- Cook the pork rolls; cook each side for 2 minutes.

- Bake in the oven at 350ºF for 25 minutes.

- In a bowl, mix the cabbage with olive oil, vinegar, and salt.

- Serve with the meat.

Beef Zucchini Lasagna

6 Servings

Preparation Time: 1 hour

Ingredients

- 1 ½ lb ground beef
- 3 large zucchinis, sliced lengthwise
- 1 ½ cup mozzarella cheese, shredded
- 2 tbsp olive oil
- 4 cloves garlic
- 2 medium white onion, chopped
- 4 tomatoes, chopped
- Salt and black pepper to taste
- 3 tsp sweet paprika
- 1 tsp dried thyme
- 1 tsp dried basil

Directions

- Preheat the oven to 370ºF.
- Cook the beef for 4 minutes in olive oil over medium heat.
- Top the beef with onion, garlic, tomatoes, salt, paprika, and pepper.
- Stir and cook for 5 minutes.
- In a baking pan, Lay ⅓ of the zucchini slices.

- Top the slices with ⅓ of the beef mixture and repeat the layering process two more times with the same quantities.

- Season the layers with basil and thyme.

- Spread the mozzarella cheese on top.

- Bake lasagna for 35 minutes.

- Remove the lasagna and let it cool for 10 minutes before serving.

Stuffed Eggplants with cheddar and beef

6 servings

Preparation time: 30 minutes

Ingredients

- 3 eggplants
- 3tbsp olive oil
- 2 lb ground beef
- 2 cup yellow cheddar cheese, grated
- 2 roasted red pepper, chopped
- 2 tbsp dill, chopped
- 2 medium red onion, chopped
- Pink salt and black pepper to taste

Directions

- Preheat oven to 350ºF.

- Trim the eggplants and cut them in half lengthwise.

- Scoop out the pulp from each half to make shells.

- Chop the pulp.

- Heat oil in a pan over medium heat. Add the ground beef, red onion, and eggplant pulp and season with salt and pepper, and cook for 6 minutes.

- Spoon the beef into the eggplant shells and sprinkle with cheddar cheese.

- Place on a greased baking pan and cook to melt the cheese for 15 minutes until eggplant is tender. Serve warm topped with dill.

Grilled lemony Lamb

6 servings

Preparation time: 25 minutes

Ingredients

- 2 lb lamb chops
- Salt and black pepper to taste
- 3 tbsp olive oil

For Sauce

- 1 cup olive oil
- 2 tsp red pepper flakes
- 3 tbsp lemon juice
- 3 tbsp lemon zest
- 1 cup parsley
- 1 tsp smoked paprika
- 3 tbsp fresh mint
- 4 pressed garlic cloves

Directions

- Rub lamb with olive oil, pepper, and salt.
- Preheat the grill to medium heat.
- Grill the lamb chops per side for about 3 minutes.
- Whisk together the sauce ingredients in a bowl.
- Serve the lamb topped with sauce.

Salmon with Sour Cream and Parmesan

6 Serving

Preparation Time: 25 minutes

Ingredients

- 2 cup sour cream
- Pink Salt and black pepper to taste
- 5 salmon steaks
- 2 tbsp fresh dill, chopped
- 1 lemon, zested and juiced
- 1 cup Parmesan cheese, grated

Directions

- Preheat oven to 400ºF.

- In a bowl, mix the sour cream, lemon zest, dill, juice, salt, and pepper.

- Season the fish with salt and black pepper, sprinkle lemon juice on both sides of the fish and arrange them on a wizened baking sheet.

- Spread the sour cream mixture on each fish and intersperse it with Parmesan cheese.

- Bake the fish for 15 minutes and after broil the top for 2 minutes with a close watch for a nice brown color.

- Plate the fish and serve with buttery green beans.

Mussels in Coconut Curry

4 Servings

Preparation Time: 25 minutes

Ingredients

- 2 tbsp minced garlic
- 1 cups coconut milk
- 1 cups dry white wine
- 1 tsp red curry powder
- 2 lb mussels, cleaned, de-bearded
- ½ cup minced shallots
- ½ cup coconut oil
- ½ cup chopped green onions
- ½ cup chopped parsley

Directions

- Pour the wine into a saucepan and cook over medium heat the shallots and garlic for 5 minutes.

- Stir in the red curry powder and coconut milk and cook for 3 minutes. Add the mussels and steam for 7 minutes or until their shells are opened.

- Then, use a slotted spoon to remove to a bowl leaving the sauce in the pan.

- At this point discard any closed mussels.

- Stir the coconut oil into the sauce, turn the heat off, and stir in the green onions and parsley.

- Serve the mussels immediately with a butternut squash mash.

Sesame Tofu Skewers with Kale Salad

Preparation Time: 30 minutes + marinating time

Ingredients

- 2 lemon, juiced
- 6 tbsp sugar-free soy sauce
- 5 tbsp coconut flour
- 16 oz firm tofu, cut into strips
- 5 tsp sesame oil
- 1 cup sesame seeds

Kale salad

- 2 white onion, thinly sliced
- 3 cloves garlic, minced
- 2 cup sliced white mushrooms
- 5 cups kale, chopped
- 3 tbsp olive oil
- 2 tsp fresh rosemary, chopped
- Salt and black pepper to taste
- 2 tbsp balsamic vinegar

Directions

- In a bowl, mix sesame oil, coconut flour and lemon juice, soy sauce.

- Stick the tofu on skewers, height-wise. Place onto a plate, pour the soy sauce mixture over, and turn in the sauce to coat.

- Cover the dish with cling film and marinate for 2 hours in the fridge. Heat a griddle pan over high heat.

- Roll the tofu skewers in the sesame seeds for a generous coat.

- Grill the tofu in the griddle pan until golden brown on both sides, about 12 minutes in total. Heat the olive oil in a skillet over medium heat and sauté onion to begin browning for 5 minutes with continuous stirring. Add in the mushrooms, garlic, rosemary, salt, pepper, and balsamic vinegar. Continue cooking for 5 minutes.

- Put the kale in a salad bowl. Pour the onion mixture over and toss well.

- Serve the tofu skewers with the warm kale salad and a peanut butter dipping sauce.

Vegetable cream Stew

6 servings

Preparation time: 25 minutes

Ingredients

- 2 cups heavy cream
- 3 tbsp ghee
- 1 tbsp onion-garlic puree
- 2 medium carrots, chopped
- 1 head cauliflower, cut into florets
- 2 cups green beans, halved
- Salt and black pepper to taste
- 1 cup water

Directions

- Melt the ghee in a pan over medium heat.
- Sauté onion-garlic puree to be fragrant for about 2 minutes.
- Stir in carrots, cauliflower, and green beans for 5 minutes.
- Season the veggies with salt and black pepper.
- Pour in the water, stir again, and cook on low heat for 15 minutes.
- Mix in the heavy cream turns the heat off.
- Serve the stew with almond flour bread.

Vegan Colorful Soup

4 servings

Preparation time: 25 minutes

Ingredients

- 1 tsp olive oil
- 1 red onion, chopped
- 2 cloves garlic, minced
- 1 cup collard greens, chopped
- Salt and black pepper to taste
- 2 thyme sprigs, chopped
- 1 tbsp white miso paste
- ½ cup arugula
- 1 celery stalk, chopped
- 1 head broccoli, chopped
- 1 carrot, sliced
- 1 cup spinach, torn into pieces
- 1 rosemary sprig, chopped
- 2 bay leaves
- 5 cups vegetable stock
- 1tomatoes, chopped
- 1 cup almond milk

Directions

- Place a large pot over medium heat and warm oil.

- Sauté carrot, celery, onion, broccoli, garlic until soft, about 5 minutes.

- Place in spinach, salt, rosemary, tomatoes, bay leaves, black pepper, collard greens, thyme, and vegetable stock.

- Bring to a boil and simmer the mixture for 15 minutes while the lid is slightly open.

- Stir in white miso paste, arugula, and almond milk, and cook for 5 more minutes.

Brunch Keto Recipes

Chicken Kebabs

4 servings

Preparation time: 20 minutes + marinade time

Ingredients

- 2 lb chicken breasts, cubed
- 2 tbsp five-spice powder
- 2 tbsp granulated sweetener
- 1 tbsp fish sauce
- 3 tbsp sesame oil
- 1 cup red bell peppers, chopped

Directions

- In a bowl mix the sesame oil, fish sauce, five-spice powder, and granulated sweetener.
- Add in the chicken and coat well.
- Marinate the chicken for 1 hour in the fridge.
- Preheat the grill.
- Thread the chicken and bell peppers onto skewers.
- Grill for 3 minutes per side.
- Serve warm with steamed broccoli.

Shrimp Sushi Rolls

6 servings

Preparation Time: 10 minutes

Ingredients

- 6 hand roll nori sheets
- 3 cups cooked and chopped shrimp
- 1 ½ tbsp sriracha sauce
- 1 cucumber, julienned
- ½ cup mayonnaise
- ½ cup sugar-free soy sauce

Directions

- In a bowl add shrimp, mayonnaise, cucumber, and sriracha sauce and mix well.
- Layout a single nori sheet on a flat surface and spread about 1/4 of the shrimp mixture.
- Roll the nori sheet as desired.
- Repeat with the other ingredients.
- Serve with sugar-free soy sauce.

Tomato and Avocado Burritos

6 servings

Preparation time: 10 minutes

Ingredients

- 2 cups tomato herb salsa
- 3 avocados, peeled, pitted, sliced
- 3 cups cauli rice
- 8 low carb tortillas
- 2 ½ cups sour cream sauce

Directions

- Pour the cauli rice into a bowl.
- Soften the cauli rice with little water in the microwave for about 2 minutes.
- Spread the sour cream all over the tortillas and distribute the salsa on top.
- Top with cauli rice and scatter the avocado evenly on top.
- Fold and tuck the burritos and cut them into two. Serve.

Vegetarian patties Burgers

3 servings

Preparation time: 20 minutes

Ingredients

- 1 garlic clove, minced3 eggs, fried
- 3 low carb buns
- 3 tbsp mayonnaise
- 3 lettuce leaves
- 3 portobello mushrooms, sliced
- 1 tbsp coconut oil, melted
- 1 tbsp fresh basil, chopped
- Salt to taste

Directions

- Combine the melted coconut oil, garlic, basil, and salt in a bowl.
- Add the mushrooms in the sauce and toss to coat.
- Form into burger patties.
- Preheat the grill to medium heat. Grill the patties for 2 minutes per side.
- Cut the buns in half.
- Add the lettuce, mushrooms, eggs, and mayonnaise.
- Top with the other bun half and Serve.

Stuffed Mushrooms with Blue Cheese

3 servings

Preparation time: 30 minutes

Ingredients

- 1 ½ cup blue cheese, crumbled
- 6 portobello mushrooms, stems removed
- 3 cups lettuce
- 3 tbsp olive oil

Directions

- Preheat oven to 350ºF.
- Lined the baking sheet.
- Fill the mushrooms with blue cheese and place them on a sheet.
- Bake for 20 minutes.
- Serve with lettuce and drizzled olive oil on top.

Yummy Coconut Crab Patties

6 servings

Preparation Time: 15 minutes

Ingredients

- 2 lb lump crab meat
- 2 eggs, beaten
- 3 tbsp coconut flour
- 3 tbsp coconut oil
- 2 tbsp lemon juice
- 3 tsp Dijon mustard

Directions

- In a bowl, add crab meat along with eggs, flour, and lemon and mix well.
- Make patties out of the mixture.
- Melt the coconut oil in a cooking pan over medium heat.
- Add the crab patties and cook for about 2-3 minutes per side.
- Enjoy low-carb bread or fresh salad.

Blackened Fish Tacos with Slaw

Preparation Time: 20 minutes

Ingredients

- 3 tilapia fillets
- 1 tsp paprika
- 6 low carb tortillas
- 2 tbsp olive oil
- 1 tsp chili powder

For Slaw
- 1 tsp apple cider vinegar
- 2 tbsp olive oil
- 1 cup red cabbage, shredded
- 1 tbsp lemon juice
- Salt and black pepper to taste

Directions

- Season the tilapia with chili powder and paprika.
- Cook tilapia in olive oil in a skillet over medium heat until blackened or 3 minutes per side.
- Cut cooked tilapia into strips.
- Divide the tilapia evenly between the tortillas.
- Combine all slaw ingredients in a bowl and top the fish to serve.

Cranberry Chicken Wings

4 Servings

Preparation Time: 50 minutes

Ingredients

- 4 tbsp unsweetened cranberry puree
- 2 lb chicken wings
- 3 tbsp olive oil
- Salt to taste
- 4 tbsp chili sauce
- Lemon juice from 1 lemon

Directions

- Preheat oven to 400ºF.
- In a bowl, mix cranberry puree, olive oil, salt, chili sauce, and lemon juice.
- Add in the wings and toss to coat.
- Place the chicken under the broiler and cook for 45 minutes, turning once halfway.
- Remove the chicken after and serve warm with a cranberry dipping sauce.

Cauli Cheesy Fritters

6 Servings

Preparation Time: 35 minutes

Ingredients

- 2 lb grated cauliflower
- 1 cup Parmesan cheese, grated
- 1 onion, chopped
- ½ tsp baking powder
- 1 cup almond flour
- 3 eggs
- 1 tsp lemon juice
- 3 tbsp olive oil
- 1 tsp salt

Directions

- Place the cauliflower in a bowl and season with salt.
- Add in all ingredients.
- Mix with your hands to combine well.
- Place a pan over medium heat and heat olive oil.
- Shape patties out of the cauliflower mixture.
- Fry in batches for about 3 minutes per side until golden around the edges and set.
- Serve warm with your favorite sauce.

Dinner Keto Recipes

Tangy Ratatouille

4 Servings

Preparation Time: 47 minutes

Ingredients

- 1 eggplant, chopped
- 2 zucchinis, chopped
- 1 red onion, diced
- ½ cup fresh basil leaves, chopped
- 2 sprigs thyme
- 1 tbsp balsamic vinegar
- ½ (15 oz) can tomatoes, diced
- 1 red bell peppers, cut into chunks
- 1 yellow bell pepper, cut into chunks
- 3 garlic cloves, sliced
- 2 tbsp olive oil
- ½ lemon, zested

Directions

- Heat the olive oil over medium heat in a casserole pot.
- Sauté the eggplants, zucchinis, and bell peppers for about 5 minutes.
- Spoon out the veggies into a bowl.
- In the same pan, sauté garlic, onions, and thyme for 5 minutes until fragrant.

- Add in the tomatoes, balsamic vinegar, basil, salt, and black pepper to taste.

- Add cooked veggies to the pan.

- Mix the veggies with sauce well and cover the pot.

- Cook the veggies on low heat for a maximum of 30 minutes.

- Stir in the remaining basil leaves, lemon zest, and adjust the seasoning.

- Turn the heat off. Plate the ratatouille and serve with some low-carb bread.

Pork Meatballs in Pasta Sauce

4 Servings

Preparation Time: 45 minutes

Ingredients

- ½ cup coconut milk
- 2 eggs, beaten
- 1 lb ground pork
- ½ cup Parmesan cheese, grated
- ½ cup asiago cheese, grated
- 1 tbsp olive oil
- ½ cup pork rinds, crushed
- 2 cloves garlic, minced
- Salt and black pepper to taste
- 2 jars sugar-free marinara sauce
- 1 cup Italian blend kinds of cheeses
- 3 tbsp fresh basil, chopped

Directions

- Preheat oven to 400ºF.

- Add the coconut milk and pork rinds to a bowl and mix.

- Mix in the ground pork, garlic, asiago cheese, Parmesan cheese, eggs, salt, and pepper with the rinds.

- Form balls of the mixture and place them in a greased baking pan.

- Bake in the oven for 20 minutes. Transfer the meatballs to a plate.

- Pour half of the marinara sauce into the baking pan.

- Place the meatballs back in the pan and pour in the remaining marinara sauce.

- Sprinkle with the Italian blend cheeses and drizzle with olive oil.

- Cover the pan with foil and put it in the oven.

- Bake for 10 minutes. After, remove the foil, and cook for 5 minutes.

- Take out the pan and garnish with basil.

- Serve on a bed of squash spaghetti.

One-pan Turkey with Bell Pepper

6 Servings

Preparation Time: 25 minutes

Ingredients

- 2 lb turkey breast, skinless, boneless
- 1 tsp ground coriander
- 1 green bell pepper, seeded, sliced
- 1 red bell pepper, seeded, sliced
- 1 onion, sliced
- 1 tsp garlic powder
- 1 tsp chili powder
- 1 tsp cumin
- 2 tbsp lime juice
- 1 tbsp fresh cilantro, chopped
- 1 avocado, sliced
- 2 limes, cut into wedges
- Salt and black pepper to taste
- 1 tsp sweet paprika
- 3 tbsp coconut oil

Directions

- In a bowl, add lime juice, coriander, paprika, salt, chili powder, cumin, garlic powder, and black pepper and mix well.

- Slice the turkey meat into strips and add them to the spices bowl.

- Toss to coat and let sit for 10 minutes to marinate.

- Warm the coconut oil in a pan over medium heat.

- Cook turkey from each side for 3-5 minutes and remove to a plate.

- In the same pan, stir the onion and bell peppers, cook for 6 minutes.

- Take the turkey back to the pan and stir well.

- Shower with cilantro.

- Serve topped with lime wedges and avocado slices and enjoy.

Sirloin Steak with Diane Sauce

4 Servings

Preparation Time: 25 minutes

Ingredients

For Sirloin steak

- 1 lb sirloin steak
- 1 tsp olive oil
- Salt and black pepper to taste

For Diane Sauce

- 2 tbsp butter
- 1 tbsp Dijon mustard
- 2 tbsp Worcestershire sauce
- ¼ cup whiskey
- 1 cups heavy cream
- 1 tbsp olive oil
- 1 clove garlic, minced
- 1 cup sliced porcini mushrooms
- 1 small onion, finely diced

Directions

- Put a grill pan over high heat.
- Brush the steak with oil, salt, and pepper.
- Rub the seasoning into the meat with your hands.

- Cook the steak for 4 minutes on each side for medium-rare texture.

- Rest the steak for about 4 minutes and then slice on chopping board and reserve the juice.

- Heat the oil in a pan over medium heat and sauté the onion for 3 minutes.

- Add the butter, garlic, and mushrooms, and cook for 2 minutes.

- Add the Worcestershire sauce, the reserved meat juice, and mustard and cook for 1 minute.

- Pour in the whiskey and cook for 1 minute until the sauce reduces by half. Swirl the pan and add the cream.

- Simmer the sauce to thicken for about 3 minutes.

- Spoon the sauce over the steaks slices and serve with celeriac mash.

Cabbage Slaw with Tofu Sandwich

6 servings

Preparation Time: 10 minutes + marinating time

Ingredients

- 1 lb firm tofu, sliced
- 6 zero carb buns
- 1 tbsp olive oil

For Marinade
- 2 tsp chopped thyme
- 1 habanero pepper, minced
- 3 green onions, thinly sliced
- Salt and black pepper to taste
- 2 tsp allspice
- 1 tbsp erythritol
- 2 cloves garlic
- ¼ cup olive oil

For Slaw
- ½ tsp swerve sugar
- 2 tbsp white vinegar
- 1 tsp Italian seasoning
- 1 small cabbage, shredded
- 1 carrot, grated
- ½ red onion, grated
- ¼ cup olive oil
- 1 tsp Dijon mustard
- Salt and black pepper to taste

Directions

- Make the marinade by blending the allspice, salt, black pepper, erythritol, thyme, habanero, green onions, garlic, and olive oil in a food processor for a minute.

- Pour the mixture into a bowl and put in the tofu.

- Gently toss to coat. Place in the fridge to marinate for about 4 hours.

- In a large bowl, add the white vinegar, swerve sugar, olive oil, mustard, Italian seasoning, salt, and pepper and mix well.

- Stir in the cabbage, carrot, and onion and place it in the refrigerator to chill.

- Over medium heat adds oil to a pan and cook marinated tofu until brown on both sides in about 6 minutes.

- Toss the low-carb buns for crisp.

- Add the tofu with the crispy slaw on top in form of a sandwich and serve with sweet chili sauce.

Hoki fish with Almond Bread

6 servings

Preparation Time: 50 minutes

Ingredients

- 6eggs
- 6 tbsp almond flour
- 1 onion, sliced
- 3 cups sour cream
- 2 cup flaked smoked Hoki, boneless
- 2 cup cubed Hoki fillets, cubed
- 1 tbsp chopped parsley
- 1 cup pork rinds, crushed
- 1 cup grated cheddar cheese
- Salt and black pepper to taste
- 2 tbsp butter

Directions

- Boil the eggs for 10 minutes, peel the shells and chop them.

- Melt the butter in a pan and sauté the onion for 4 minutes.

- Stir in the almond flour to form a roux.

- Turn the heat back on and cook the roux until golden brown and stir in the sour cream until the mixture is smooth.

- Season with salt and pepper and stir in the parsley.

- Preheat oven to 360ºF.

- Spread the smoked and cubed fish on a greased baking dish, sprinkle the eggs on top, and spoon the sauce over.

- In a bowl, mix pork rinds and cheddar cheese and spread over the sauce.

- Bake the casserole in the oven for 20 minutes until the top is golden and the sauce and cheese are bubbly.

- Remove the bake after and serve with a steamed green vegetable mix.

Salmon in Creamy Sauce

4 Servings

Preparation Time: 15 minutes

Ingredients

- 4 salmon fillets
- 2 tsp dried tarragon
- 2 tsp dried dill
- 6 tbsp butter
- ½ cup heavy cream
- Salt and black pepper to taste

Directions

- Season the salmon with tarragon and dill.

- Warm butter in a pan over medium heat.

- Add salmon and cook for 4 minutes on both sides.

- In the same pan, add the remaining dill and tarragon and cook for 30 seconds to infuse the flavors.

- Whisk in the heavy cream, season with salt and black pepper, and cook for the other 2-3 minutes.

- Serve the salmon topped with the sauce.

Lamb Chops in White Wine

4 servings

Preparation Time: 1 hour 10 minutes

Ingredients

- 4 lamb chops
- ½ tsp sage
- ½ tsp thyme
- 1 onion, sliced
- 2 garlic cloves, minced
- 2 tbsp olive oil
- ½ cup white wine
- Salt and black pepper to taste

Directions

- Heat the olive oil in a pan. Cook onion and garlic for 3 minutes until soft.
- Rub the thyme and sage over the lamb chops.
- Cook it in the pan for about 3 minutes per side. Set aside.
- Pour the white wine and 1 cup of water into the pan and bring the mixture to a boil.
- Cook until the liquid is reduced by half, about 5 minutes.
- Add in the chops, reduce the heat, and let simmer for 1 hour and Serve hot.

Grilled Beef with Vegetables

6 Servings

Preparation Time: 30 minutes

Ingredients

- 6 sirloin steaks
- 3 tbsp olive oil
- 3 tbsp balsamic vinegar

Vegetables

- 1 lb asparagus, trimmed
- 1 cup green beans
- 1 cup snow peas
- 1 red bell pepper, cut into strips
- 1 orange bell pepper, cut into strips
- 1 medium red onion, quartered

Directions

- Set a grill pan over high heat.
- In separate bowls put the beef in one and the vegetables in another.
- Mix salt, pepper, olive oil, and balsamic vinegar in a small bowl and pour half of the mixture over the beef and the other half over the vegetables.
- Coat the ingredients in both bowls with the sauce.
- Place the steaks in the grill pan and sear both sides for 2-3 minutes each.

- When done, remove the beef onto a plate; set it aside.

- Pour the vegetables and marinade in the pan and cook for 5 minutes, turning once.

- Share the vegetables into plates. Top with beef, drizzle the sauce from the pan all over and serve.

Beef Meatloaf with mushrooms

6 Servings

Preparation Time: 1 hour and 15 minutes

Ingredients

- 1 ½ pounds ground beef
- ¼ cup chopped onions
- ¼ cup almond flour
- 1 garlic cloves, minced
- ½ cup sliced mushrooms
- 2 eggs
- ¼ tsp pepper
- 1 tbsp chopped parsley
- ¼ cup chopped bell peppers
- ½ cup grated Parmesan cheese
- 1 tsp balsamic vinegar
- 1 tsp salt

For Glaze

- ½ cups balsamic vinegar
- ½ tbsp sweetener
- ½ tbsp sugar-free ketchup

Directions

- In a large bowl, combine all meatloaf.

- Press the mixture into a greased loaf pans.

- Bake in the oven for 30 minutes at 370ºF.

- Over medium heat, combine all the glaze ingredients in a cooking pan.

- Simmer the glaze for 20 minutes until the glaze is thickened.

- Pour ¼ cup of the glaze over the meatloaf.

- Put the meatloaf back in the oven and cook for 20 more minutes.
- Serve with the remaining glaze.

Dessert Keto Recipes

Chocolaty Marshmallows

6 Servings

Preparation Time: 30 minutes

Ingredients

- 2 tbsp unsweetened cocoa powder
- ½ tsp vanilla extract
- ½ cup swerve sugar
- 1 tbsp xanthan gum
- A pinch Salt
- ½ tsp gelatin powder

Directions

- Line the bread pan with parchment paper and grease with cooking spray.
- Mix the xanthan gum with water and pour it into a saucepan. Add in the swerve sugar, 2 tbsp of water, and salt.
- Place the pan over medium heat and bring the mixture to a boil.
- Simmer on low heat for 7 minutes.
- Cover the gelatin with cold water in a small bowl for 5 minutes and stir.
- When the gelatin dissolves, pour the remaining water into a small bowl and heat it in the microwave for 30 seconds.

- Mix in cocoa powder and mix it into the gelatin.

- When the sugar solution has hit the right temperature, gradually pour it directly into the gelatin mixture while continuously whisking.

- Beat for 10 minutes to get a light and fluffy consistency.

- Stir in the vanilla and pour the Marshmallow blend into the loaf pan.

- Let the marshmallows set for 3 hours and then use an oiled knife to cut them into cubes; place them on a plate.

- Mix the remaining cocoa powder and confectioner's sugar.

- Sift it over the marshmallows and enjoy a yummy treat.

Dark Chocolate Mousse topped with Stewed Plums

4 Servings

Preparation Time: 45 minutes + cooling time

Ingredients

- 8 eggs, separated into yolks and whites
- 12 oz unsweetened chocolate
- 2 tbsp salt
- ¾ cup swerve sugar
- ½ cup olive oil
- 3 tbsp brewed coffee

Stewed plums

- ½ stick cinnamon
- Plums pitted and halved
- ½ cup swerve sugar
- ½ cup water
- ½ lemon, juiced

Directions

- Melt the chocolate in the microwave.
- In another bowl, whisk the yolks with swerve until a pale yellow color has formed. Add salt, olive oil, and coffee and beat.
- Mix in the melted chocolate until smooth.

- In another bowl, whisk the whites with a hand mixer until a soft peak has formed.

- Sprinkle the remaining swerve over and gently fold in with a spatula. Fetch a tablespoon full of the chocolate mixture and fold in to combine.

- Pour in the remaining chocolate mixture and whisk to mix. Pour the mousse into 6 ramekins, cover with plastic wrap, and refrigerate overnight.

- The following day, pour water, swerve sugar, cinnamon, and lemon juice in a saucepan and bring to a simmer for 3 minutes, occasionally stirring to ensure the swerve has dissolved and the syrup has formed.

- Add the plums and poach in the sweetened water for 18 minutes until soft.

- Turn the heat off and discard the cinnamon stick.

- Spoon a plum with syrup on each mousse ramekin and serve.

Cheesecake with coconut cream

6 servings

Preparation Time: 30 minutes + cooling time

Ingredients

For Crust

- 1 egg whites
- ¼ cup erythritol
- 1 ½ cups desiccated coconut
- 1 tsp coconut oil
- ¼ cup melted butter

For Filling

- 1 tbsp lemon juice
- 3 oz raspberries
- 1 cups erythritol
- ½ cup whipped cream
- Zest of 1 lemon
- 12 oz cream cheese

Directions

- Grease the pan with coconut oil and line with parchment paper.
- Preheat oven to 350ºF.
- Mix crust ingredients and pour the crust into the pan. Bake for about 25 minutes; let cool.

- Beat the cream cheese with an electric mixer until soft.

- Add the lemon juice, zest, and erythritol.

- Fold the whipped cream into the cheese cream mixture.

- Fold in the raspberries gently.

- Spoon the filling into the baked and cooled crust.

- Place in the fridge for 4 hours and serve in slices.

Cheesecake Slices with Passion fruit jelly

6 Servings

Preparation Time: 15 minutes + cooling time

Ingredients

- 2 cup crushed almond biscuits
- 1 cup melted butter

For Filling

- 4-6 tbsp cold water
- 1 tbsp gelatin powder
- 2 cups cream cheese
- 1 cup swerve sugar
- 2 whipping cream
- 1 tsp vanilla bean paste

Passion fruit jelly

- 2 cup passion fruit pulp
- ½ cup swerve confectioner's sugar
- 1 tsp gelatin powder
- ¼ cup water, room temperature

Directions

- Mix the crushed biscuits and butter in a bowl. Spoon into a spring-form pan, and use the back of the spoon to level at the bottom. Set aside in the fridge.

- Put the cream cheese, swerve sugar, and vanilla paste into a bowl, and use the hand mixer to whisk until smooth; set aside.

- Cover the gelatin with cold water in a small bowl. Let dissolve for 5 minutes.

- Pour the gelatin liquid along with the whipping cream in the cheese mixture and fold gently.

- Remove the spring-form pan from the refrigerator and pour over the mixture. Return to the fridge.

- For the passion fruit jelly: add 2 tbsp of cold water and sprinkle 1 tsp of gelatin powder.

- Let dissolve for 5 minutes. Pour the confectioner's sugar and ¼ cup of water into it. Mix and stir in passion fruit pulp.

- Remove the cake again and pour the jelly over it.

- Swirl the pan to make the jelly level up.

- Place the pan back into the fridge to cool for 2 hours.

- When completely set, remove, and unlock the spring-pan.

- Lift the pan from the cake and slice the dessert.

Chocolate Cakes with Almond Flour

4 Servings

Preparation Time: 25 minutes

Ingredients

- ½ cup almond flour
- A pinch of salt
- A pinch of ground cloves
- ¼ cup xylitol
- 1 tsp baking powder
- ½ tsp baking soda
- 1 tsp cinnamon, ground
- ½ cup butter, melted
- ½ cup buttermilk
- 1 egg
- 1 tsp pure almond extract

For the Frosting:

- 1 cup heavy cream
- 1 cup dark chocolate, flaked

Directions

- Preheat oven to 360ºF.
- Mix the cloves, almond flour, baking powder, salt, baking soda, xylitol, and cinnamon in a bowl.
- In a separate bowl, combine the almond extract, butter, egg, and buttermilk.

- Combine the wet mixture into the dry mix.

- Pour the batter into the greased baking pan and bake for 17 minutes.

- On medium heat, warm heavy cream for 2 minutes.

- Fold in the chocolate flakes into the cream and stir until all the chocolate melts.

- let cool then gnash and spread the top of the cake with the frosting.

Keto Drinks

Coconut and Lychee Lassi

6 Servings

Preparation Time: 30 minutes + cooling time

Ingredients

- 3 cups lychee pulp, seeded
- 3 cups coconut milk
- 6 tsp swerve sugar
- 2 tbsp toasted coconut shavings
- 2 limes, zested and juiced
- 1 ½ cups plain yogurt
- 1 lemongrass, white part only, torn
- A pinch of salt

Directions

- Add the lychee pulp, coconut milk, and lemongrass, swerve sugar, and lime zest.
- Stir and bring to boil on medium heat for 2 minutes.
- Simmer the mix for 1 minute.
- Turn the heat off and cool the mix for 15 minutes.
- Remove the lemongrass.
- Pour the mixture into a blender.
- Add in the yogurt, salt, and lime juice and process the ingredients until smooth, about 60 seconds.
- Pour into a jug and refrigerate for 2 hours until cold.

Chocolate and Mint Protein Shake

6 Servings

Preparation Time: 4 minutes

Ingredients

- 2 avocado, pitted, peeled, sliced
- 2 cup coconut milk, chilled
- 6 mint leaves + extra to garnish
- 5 cups flax milk, chilled
- 4 tsp unsweetened cocoa powder
- 3 tbsp erythritol
- 1 tbsp low carb Protein powder
- Whipping cream for topping

Directions

- Add milk, avocado, coconut milk, mint leaves, cocoa powder, erythritol, and protein powder into a blender,
- Blend them for 1 minute until smooth.
- Pour into serving glasses, with some whipping cream on top, and garnish with mint leaves.

Basil and Strawberry Lemonade

6 Servings

Preparation Time: 3 minutes

Ingredients

- 1 cup fresh lemon juice
- 1 cup fresh basil
- 6 cups water
- 24 strawberries, leaves removed
- 1cup swerve sugar
- Crushed Ice
- Halved strawberries to garnish
- Basil leaves to garnish

Directions

- Add crushed ice into 6 serving glasses and set aside.
- In a pitcher, add the water, lemon juice, basil, strawberries, and swerve.
- Insert the blender and process the lemonade for 30 seconds.
- The mixture should be pink, and the basil finely chopped.
- Drop 2 strawberry halves and some basil in each glass and serve immediately.

Turmeric and Cinnamon Latte

6 Servings

Preparation Time: 7 minutes

Ingredients

- 2 cup brewed coffee
- 1 tsp turmeric powder
- 6 cups almond milk
- 1 tsp cinnamon powder
- 2 tbsp erythritol
- Cinnamon sticks to garnish

Directions

- Add the almond milk, coffee, turmeric cinnamon powder, and erythritol in a blender.
- Blend the ingredients at medium speed for 45 seconds.
- Pour the mixture into a saucepan.
- Set the pan over low heat and heat through for 5 minutes; do not boil.
- Keep swirling the pan to prevent boiling.
- Turn the heat off, and serve in latte cups, with a cinnamon stick in each one.

CPSIA information can be obtained
at www.ICGtesting.com
Printed in the USA
BVHW061904300321
603711BV00003BA/349